D0938446

# SOCIETY'S SISTERS

## STORIES OF WOMEN WHO FOUGHT FOR SOCIAL JUSTICE IN AMERICA

CATHERINE GOURLEY

TWENTY-FIRST CENTURY BOOKS    BROOKFIELD, CONNECTICUT

Front cover photographs courtesy of Brown Brothers and Library of Congress (inset). Back cover photographs courtesy of Department of Special Collections, University of Chicago Library (Ida B. Wells-Burnett); Jane Addams Memorial Collection, University of Illinois at Chicago (Jane Addams); Library of Congress (Mary Church); The Schlesinger Library, Radcliffe Institute, Harvard University (Alice Hamilton); Brown Brothers (Frances Willard and Alice Paul).

Photographs courtesy of Carnegie Library of Pittsburgh, Pennsylvania Department: pp. 1, 9; Brown Brothers: pp. 5, 12, 15, 20, 25 (bottom), 30, 44, 46, 52, 67, 70 (both), 71, 73, 77, 83; Getty Images: pp. 6 (Hulton/Archive), 22 (Hulton/Archive), 25 (top: © George Eastman House); Jane Addams Memorial Collection, University of Illinois at Chicago: p. 17 (left); The New York Public Library, Schomburg Center for Research in Black Culture: pp. 17 (right: #SC-CN-90-0749), 56 (bottom: #SC-CN-89-0284); Library of Congress: pp. 28, 63, 67 (inset); © State Historical Society of Wisconsin: p. 32 (Image #WHi (x3) 52141); © Corbis: pp. 36 (Bettmann), 39, 79; The Schlesinger Library, Radcliffe Institute, Harvard University: pp. 40, 41; Special Collections, Willard Library: p. 45; Ohio Historical Society: p. 51 (#SC 5354); Birmingham Public Library: p. 56 (top); Department of Special Collections, University of Chicago Library: p. 59

Library of Congress Cataloging-in-Publication Data

Gourley, Catherine, 1950–
Society's sisters : stories of women who fought for social justice in America / Catherine Gourley.
p. cm.
Summary: Profiles nineteenth-century women who overcame the disadvantage of being female in order to change the society in which they lived, by promoting temperance, child labor laws, health care, and other causes. Includes bibliographical references and index.
ISBN 0-7613-2865-3 (lib. bdg.)
1. Women social reformers—United States—History—19th century—Juvenile literature. 2. Women political activists—United States—History—19th century—Juvenile literature. 3. Social justice—United States—History—19th century—Juvenile literature. 4. United States—Social conditions—19th century—Juvenile literature. 5. United States—Moral conditions—Juvenile literature. [1. Women social reformers. 2. Women political activists. 3. Social justice—History—19th century. 4. United States—Social conditions—19th century. 5. United States—Moral conditions.] I. Title.
HQ1418 .G68 2003    303.48'4'0973—dc21    2003000560

Published by Twenty-First Century Books
A Division of The Millbrook Press, Inc.
2 Old New Milford Road
Brookfield, Connecticut 06804
www.millbrookpress.com

Printed in the United States of America
1 3 5 4 2

# CONTENTS

*A match factory worker*

An 1871 engraving showing brickyard children being
paid for their labors at an inn.

# THE HAVES AND THE HAVE-NOTS

**W**hen Florence Kelley was growing up in Philadelphia in the 1860s, she often rode a horse-drawn streetcar to school. One morning the car passed a factory building where little girls huddled in the cold outside the doors. The girls reminded Florence of drawings in a book her father had given her. Those pictures showed children nine and ten years old laboring in the brickyards of England. "They looked like trolls and gnomes, with crooked legs and bent backs," Florence remembered. The streetcar continued on its way, but the memory of those slump-shouldered factory girls of Philadelphia stayed with Florence a very long time.

Florence's father was William Kelley, a United States congressman and one of the wealthiest men in Philadelphia. He had given Florence the book on child labor to teach her about others who were less fortunate than she. The child's grandparents disapproved. "You are darkening her mind with dismal ideas," they said. Kelley was a Quaker. He believed in social justice for the poor and the weak. He saw no danger in opening his young daughter's eyes to the real world around her.[1]

Perhaps that was why sometime later the congressman took Florence with him on a visit to a steelmaking plant in Pittsburgh. They arrived at two in the morning. No doubt Florence was excited to be her father's companion on this important visit. Once she was inside, however, her excitement quickened to terror. The air was white hot with steam. Giant blast furnaces were melting iron in huge brick-lined buckets. Men, bare-chested and sweating, operated cranes that poured buckets of liquid metal into molds. The steelmaking process fascinated the congressman. It represented progress. Pennsylvania's steel industry could make America a strong and prosperous nation.

Florence turned away from the furnaces. That's when she saw the boys. They were "smaller than myself," she said, "carrying pails of water and tin dippers, from which men drank eagerly." Two in the morning was a forbidden hour for an upper-class child like Florence to be awake and out of bed. It was not forbidden for these children of poor working families. Just as Florence had not forgotten the sight of the factory girls along the horsecar line in Philadelphia, she would not soon forget the soot-faced boys of Pittsburgh.[2]

America in the latter half of the nineteenth century was a country of haves and have-nots. The sons and daughters of rich men lived in mansions with plate glass windows and lace curtains. Across town, the children of poor families crowded inside tenement buildings that had few or no windows at all. Frances Willard was a social reformer of the nineteenth century. She described the haves and have-nots in America this way:

RICH IDLERS AMUSING THEMSELVES in [the mansions of] Newport, Rhode Island, and Tuxedo, New York; poor workers burying themselves in coal mines. Young men and women riding across country after a bag that smells like a fox; old men and women picking decayed food out of garbage cans. Lap dogs driving through Central Park to take the air; children stripping tobacco stems in garrets.[3]

Much was good and right about America, but much was also unjust. The Civil War had ended and those who were once slaves were now free citizens. And yet, lynch mobs tortured and killed Negro men, women, and children. Colleges had begun to open their doors to women. As a result, more women were becoming teachers, doctors, and lawyers. And yet, women could not enter a polling place to cast a ballot. New med-

*One of the eleven blast furnaces operating in Pittsburgh during the 1870s*

ical discoveries, including the use of antiseptics to prevent infection during operations, saved lives. And yet, diseases like cholera and scarlet fever still spread through city slums. Infants by the thousands died of dysentery, especially in the hot months of summer. Not even the children of the wealthy could escape sickness. Florence Kelley grieved for five brothers and sisters who died of childhood diseases.

The progress that created new industries and grew cities in America in the nineteenth century also changed society. The first generation of women who graduated from colleges wondered *What now?* and wished for more. More independence. More responsibility. More voice in the ways of running industries and building cities. Jane Addams and Alice Hamilton, Ida B. Wells and Mary Church Terrell, Francis Willard and Alice Paul—many hundreds of women, in fact, all across the country began to question the social order of things. Why must so many infants die of disease? Why must delinquent children go to prison with adult criminals? Why did men squander their hard-earned money in saloons, returning home belligerent and abusive to their wives and children?

Women formed a sisterhood. At first, they gathered in clubs as a way to learn more about their world and each other. Soon, however, their focus shifted to making the world a better place. As one club member explained, "Women were no longer content to pass unsightly dump heaps of refuse on their way to a club meeting where they might listen to a lecture about art."[4]

The sisters rolled up their sleeves. They started kindergartens and playground programs. They investigated filthy living conditions in tenements, then wrote legislation to authorize a clean-up of the slums. Some formed settlements, or small communities, to teach poor families how to care for their infants. Others formed political parties to end war and to win for women equal rights, including the right to vote. With each struggle came social resistance and ridicule. The women did not shy away.

Alone, a woman's voice was a whisper. Together as society's sisters, their voices thundered. This is the story of those women who dared to make a difference, and in daring changed society and the conscience of America forever.

## CHAPTER ONE

# THE WOMAN'S SPHERE

The average woman knows about clothes,
the next world, children, and her domestic duties.
Let her stick to her sphere. A woman at a political caucus?
Who would see that my dinner was properly cooked, eh?

*Scribner's Monthly Magazine, October 1895*

n April 19, 1868, the New York Press Club held a lavish dinner at Delmonico's Restaurant in New York City. The dinner honored Charles Dickens. This was Dickens's second visit to America and most likely his last, for the popular British author was seriously ill.

Jane Cunningham Croly was a journalist. Her pen name was Jennie June, and her articles appeared in many magazines in New York City, Boston, and Baltimore. Her husband, David, was also an editor and writer. Both were members of the New York Press Club. However, only David received an invitation to attend the Dickens banquet.

Jane Croly attempted to purchase a ticket to the banquet, but the Press Club refused to allow women to attend even the after-dinner toasts and speeches. Finally, three days before the event, the Press Club relented. They would admit women on one condition: They must sit behind a curtain, unseen by the gentlemen in the audience and unseen, as well, by the guest of honor, Mr. Dickens.

"Whatever else she believed in," her brother, John Cunningham, said, "Jennie certainly believed in women, their instincts and capacities." And, he added, she had a "volcanic force that was terrific" if she felt she had been wronged.[1] Asking Jennie June to hide behind a curtain while her fellow journalists sat at dining tables was most certainly a wrong. Croly refused to attend the banquet, after all.

*Jane Croly is credited with establishing the first women's organization dedicated to self-improvement of its members—a revolutionary concept in her time.*

She soon turned her indignation into action. "We will form a club of our own," she declared. "We will give a banquet to ourselves, make all the speeches ourselves, and not invite a single man."

Women had organized in the past, and for very worthy purposes—to raise funds to build churches, to help clothe soldiers in the Civil War, to argue for the abolition of slavery. "But," Croly emphasized, "women have always allowed men to transact the principal part of the business for them."

Her ladies would not darn socks for soldiers or bake cakes for church socials. Nor would they gather to gossip over tea about trivial things like romance. Instead, Croly proposed a women's movement for self-improvement. She called her new club Sorosis. The word comes from the Latin *soror*, or sister. Sorosis had another meaning—a flower with many blooms. Sorosis would help women to bloom by presenting lectures and discussions on the arts and education. Sorosis would teach women to think for themselves, rather than getting their opinions from their husbands and fathers. Croly admitted the idea was not only new, "it was startling."

In 1868, a lady did not express her opinion in public if it were not in agreement with her husband's. She did not go out in public alone nor dine in fine restaurants without a male escort. Croly further stunned New York society, therefore, by holding the first meeting of Sorosis in the very place from which she had been barred on the evening of Dickens's farewell dinner.

The seeds of the women's club movement took root among the marble pillars of Delmonico's Restaurant.

## "Someone to Protect Her When I'm Gone": Margaret Fuller

A sphere is an environment, a realm. For women in the nineteenth century, it was also a specific place: the home. To understand why Sorosis was so shocking, one must first understand what nineteenth-century society believed about women and women's sphere.

One belief was that women were physically inferior to men. Another was that women were not as intelligent as men. Although a woman's strength was neither her body nor her mind, she was superior to men in one way: her moral conscience. In other words, men were strong; women were weak. Men were hard-hearted but intelligent; women were kind but dull-witted. Men were fighters in the public sphere; women were the guardians of the home sphere.

Hundreds of magazine stories reinforced these beliefs. In a book titled *The Young Lady's Counsellor*, published in 1851, Daniel Wise describes a woman's purpose in life this way:

> HER PLACE IS NOT life's great battlefields. Man belongs there. Woman must abide in the peaceful sanctuaries of home, and walk in the noiseless vales of private life. . . . There she must smile upon the husband.

There she must rear the Christian patriot and statesman, the self-denying philanthropist and the obedient citizen. There, in a word, she must form the character of the world.

Apparently, woman's place was not the classroom either.

WOMAN IS NOT INFERIOR to man, but she is different from him. . . . Her sphere is home. Here is her throne. . . . Her best education is that which fits her for this sphere; . . . those who prepare to be teachers may need to give additional attention to particular studies or accomplishments. But, even in these cases, an education for the station of the wife and the mother will be the best foundation. . . .[2]

Of course, not all nineteenth-century husbands and fathers thought their daughters and wives were dimwits. Timothy Fuller was an attorney in Massachusetts who educated his daughter Margaret at home. By the time she was ten years old, Margaret Fuller could read books in Latin. Soon she had exhausted her father's library. Nearby was Harvard University, but Harvard did not admit women as students. Nevertheless, Fuller convinced the university to allow her into its library. There, amid book stacks and gentlemen students, she continued her education on her own. A few years later, she became a teacher and a writer.

In her book *Women of the Nineteenth Century*, Margaret Fuller recorded a conversation she had overheard. A father and a mother were discussing the future of their daughter. Maria, the daughter, had eyes bright with intelligence, Fuller remembered. As Fuller listened, however, she realized the father feared rather than valued his daughter's intelligence.

*Margaret Fuller was known not only as a proponent of women's rights but also as a transcendentalist writer.*

"I SHALL NOT HAVE MARIA brought too forward. If she knows too much, she will never find a husband; superior women hardly ever can," said the father.

"Surely," said the wife, "you wish Maria to be as wise and as good as she can, whether it will help her to marriage or not."

"No," he persisted. "I want her to have a sphere and a home, and someone to protect her when I am gone."[3]

The father's words left a deep impression on Fuller. Most men were not like her father, she realized. Instead, they believed an educated woman was to be pitied. They were too independent, too outspoken, and too self-centered to attract a husband. Fuller's own opinion was that "Women must leave off asking men [for protection] and look to themselves and grow."

A law in Boston at the time forbade women from speaking in public for pay. Fuller ignored the law. She began holding seminars for women in her home. She called her meetings "conversations." Her subjects were far from the woman's sphere of child-rearing and husband-pleasing. Instead, she discussed ancient Greek civilization, the beauty of nature, and equal rights for women.

Whether in a classroom, a women's club meeting, or a parlor "conversation," education is a powerful thing. It opens windows to other worlds. As long as society kept women in the home sphere, the windows to those other worlds remained barred.

## A Woman's Discontent: Jane Addams, Ida B. Wells

Like a growing number of upper-class women after the Civil War, Jane Addams had gone to college. After graduation, she felt lost and unhappy. "I was absolutely at sea so far as any moral purpose was concerned," she said, "clinging only to the desire to live in a really living world. . . ." Later, in her autobiography, she would admit that she was "weary of myself and sick of asking, What I am and what I ought to be. . . ."[4]

Ida B. Wells felt the same vague discontent as Jane Addams. She was born the daughter of slaves in Holly Springs, Mississippi, in 1862. When she was sixteen, both her parents died in a yellow fever epidemic. As the oldest child, Ida was responsible for her orphaned brothers and sisters. She left Rust College, where she had been a student, to care for her family.

In college, Ida had read Shakespeare. Now she was teaching African American children how to read and write. Often she was not paid. Although she worried over money and whether she could make ends meet, she was also restless. She did not want flowers and romance. She did not long for a husband and children. After all, she was struggling to raise her own brothers and sisters. Still, she wrote in her diary of a yearning she felt but did not yet completely understand:

*Jane Addams was a college graduate from an upper-class family and Ida B. Wells was the daughter of slaves—but they both worked to improve the world despite the overwhelming handicap of being female.*

I AM IN correspondingly low spirits tonight as I was cheerful this morning. I don't know what's the matter with me—, I feel so dissatisfied with my life, so isolated from all my kind. I cannot or do not make friends & these fits of loneliness will come & I tire of everything. My life seems awry, the machinery out of gear & I feel there is something wrong.[5]

Other women, too, expressed a longing for something more in their lives. This anonymous woman poet published this verse in the popular *Scribner's Monthly Magazine*:

*I want—I don't know what I want;*
  *I'm tired of everything;*
*I'd like to be a queen or something—*
  *No, a bearded king,*
*With iron crown and wolfish eyes*
  *and manners fierce and bold,*
*Or else a plumed highwayman, or a*
  *paladin of old.*
*We girls are such poor creatures,*
  *slaves to circumstances and fate.*
*Denied the warrior's glory and the*
  *conqueror's splendid state.*[6]

One day soon, both Jane Addams and Ida B. Wells would find their way to a new place, a new sphere. There they would put to good use their ambition and intelligence and especially their passion. Although they did not yet know it, both women—and many more like them—were readying themselves for the warrior's glory.

## A New Ideal of Womanhood: Jane Cunningham Croly

In 1869, a year after the first Sorosis meeting at Delmonico's, membership in the club numbered eighty-three women. Although these women were upper class and professional—they were artists, writers, teachers, physicians—society did not take their association seriously. "Social tomfoolery" is how magazine editor Robert Grant described the club meetings. "To exhaust one's energies in papers or literary teas as a way to educate women . . . is as valuable to society as an ice cream maker without its crank."[7]

"The truth is," Croly argued, "the time has come when more is expected of women than before. The traditional home life is insufficient for our needs, mental and physical."[8]

The time had indeed come, for a remarkable thing was happening. Other women in other cities and other states began to form clubs, too. Some were professional women. Others were housewives or pioneers in Kansas, Missouri, Minnesota, and California. Some women, like Julia Ward Howe, who founded the New England Women's Club in Boston, were suffragists. They believed that women should have voting rights. And yet many more clubwomen did not share that radical idea. They came to club meetings because they were hungry for knowledge. The women of the Great Expectations Club in Thomaston, Maine, read great literature. The women of the Heliades Club in Chicago discussed only geography. African-American women, barred from membership in white-only women's clubs, formed their own organizations.

Every club held one thing in common: They gave women the opportunity to think and speak for themselves.

As membership in women's clubs soared into the thousands, critics became downright alarmed. This was not a fad, after all. It was a national movement. "Women's clubs are not only harmful," warned a male politician, "but harmful in a way that directly menaces the integrity of our homes." The editor of the *Boston Transcript* predicted catastrophe for the middle-class American way of life: "Homes will be ruined, children neglected, woman is straying from her sphere."[9] These clubs gave women ideas, made them strong-willed and strong-minded. Women were becoming, well . . . more like men!

Ridiculous! Croly responded. Women were certainly different from men, especially in the way they reacted to social problems. "In the heat of personal conflict, men willfully shut their eyes to oppression, corruption and vice," she charged. "It is the part of mothers who fear for their sons and of wives who love their husbands to rouse men to a sense of their short-comings."[10]

A battle had begun.

Croly's words signaled an important shift in the purpose of women's clubs. No longer was it enough to read great literature or discuss works of art. She urged clubwomen to lead public reforms.

*Representatives of the early Federation of Women's Clubs
meet at the Hotel Astor in New York City.*

THERE ARE GREAT SUBJECTS waiting for discussion; crying evils to be remedied . . . that the voice of women alone can reach.

We want legislation that will open the colleges of the land to every boy and girl in the land and give them an equal chance. . . .

We want legislation that will provide foundling hospitals for the waifs of society, asylums for the wretched mothers and the insane. . . .

We want a legislation that will at least modify the present barbarous and inhuman jail system, which makes the good bad, and the bad worse. . . .

Here is work for heart and head. Have we not women who will perform it?[11]

The answer was a resounding YES!

In 1889, twenty years after the first meeting of Sorosis, clubs across the country banded together to form the General Federation of Women's Clubs. That same year, the GFWC held its first national convention. Sixty-one clubs from across the country sent women to the meeting. At one of these meetings, an elderly woman who had listened to her fellow club members, now spoke:

I CAME HERE to listen. I never expected to speak. I never made a speech in my life . . . but I want to say that for the first time in my life I have heard women speak up and tell what they themselves want and it has done my soul good. . . . I mean to speak up more from now on. You women have lighted a fire in me that won't go out.[12]

A new ideal of womanhood was beginning to take shape.

*A Jacob Riis photograph taken in the 1890s shows three young "street arabs" huddling together to keep warm on a frosty New York day.*

## CHAPTER TWO

# THE CHILD SAVERS

Please, sir, give me but a penny
This today I've ask'd of many
And the hours go by so dreary
While I'm hungry, cold and weary.
On the streets I stand and freeze, sir.
And I'm ragged as you see, sir.
Yet there's few who look with pity
On such friendless boys as I.
There's my mother, God has taken
And my father's me forsaken.
Why then should a penny be denied
So poor a boy as I.

*Song of the "street arab," 1876*

Ten thousand orphaned and abandoned children roamed the streets of New York City in the latter half of the nineteenth century. City officials and social reformers alike called them "an army of vagabonds" or "street arabs" (nomads). Some were rowdies who banded together, with gang names like the Dead Rabbits or Bowery Boys. Many more, however, were girls and boys as young as six and seven. They were hungry and ragged, often without shoes even in winter. No one in the city quite knew what to do about them.

The youngest were beggars. They crowded near theater doors, waiting for the gentlemen and ladies to step outside to their carriages. Older children worked. Bootblacks polished shoes. "Newsies" sold newspapers on corners. Street sweepers brushed away litter and horse manure so that a lady might not soil her shoes or the hem of her skirt. The broom handle was often taller than the vagabond girl holding it. In exchange for polished shoes, a paper, or a clean place to step, the gentleman or the lady might drop a penny in the child's open hand. A palm full of pennies could buy a meal of brown bread and coffee.

The rowdies were burglars and pickpockets. They swore, stole, chewed tobacco, gambled with dice, and drank liquor, stealing that, too, when they could.

A line in a book of manners read: "A lady walks quietly through the streets, seeing and hearing nothing that she ought not to. . . ."[1] Indeed, a lady might cross the street to avoid the bawdy laughter or song from a saloon or grog shop. She might press a lacy handkerchief to her nose to check the odors of horse piss and manure rising from the gutters.

As the population of cities swelled, however, it became increasingly difficult *not* to see or smell the poverty. It was especially hard not to see the bare feet, crusted cheeks, and outstretched hands of the children. Something had to be done.

## Orphan Asylums and Protectories: Jacob Riis

Great numbers of immigrants had arrived in America in the nineteenth century. They settled first in cities in the Northeast: Boston, Trenton, Philadelphia, Pittsburgh. Diseases like typhoid fever, scarlet fever, and tuberculosis spread rapidly among people who lived in the crowded tenements. Many mothers and fathers died. Others were unable to earn enough money to feed their children. Sometimes a family member or a neighbor could help. Often, they could not.

Churches and charities had built asylums to care for these outcasts. The asylums were meant to be safe havens, protecting children from the evils of the world. But life inside was often cold and cheerless, even cruel. The superintendent and matron who ran the institutions called the children "inmates." When new children arrived, workers stripped them of their ragged clothing. They scrubbed them and often shaved their heads to kill the lice. The inmates wore uniforms of coarse material. They slept

*Newly arrived immigrant families pose for a photograph at Ellis Island, New York City's immigrant-processing center.*

*Orphanages of the nineteenth century typically had a jail-like appearance as evidenced by this playground in a New York City institution.*

in large halls called dormitories lined with a hundred or as many as two hundred cots. In some asylums, food was meager and not always nutritious. Because the institutions were charities, they relied on donations from those better off. In one Pittsburgh institution, the children received the following meals each day, nothing more:

Breakfast: coffee, bread, and a little butter

Dinner: stew, bread, water

Supper: tea, bread with spoonful of molasses on it.[2]

Bells announced mealtime, schooltime, prayer time. Those who did not answer the bells or were disobedient in some other way faced punishment. The sentence might be the loss of dinner or worse, a lashing or confinement to a cell. The really bad children, said one superintendent, were sent to reformatories.

In New York City, both the Juvenile Asylum and the Catholic Protectory housed wayward and abandoned children. In 1894, writer and social reformer Jacob Riis visited the institutions. "Both are prisons," he concluded. Most troubling for Riis was the fact that the rowdies lived side by side with children whose only crime was being poor. The superintendent admitted that the rowdies "ruined" the innocents, teaching them how to pick pockets and roll dice.

"These children were not thieves by heredity," Riis wrote. "They were made. And the manufacture goes on every day. The street and the [asylums] are the factories."[3]

Many parents did not wish to put their children in an asylum. They simply had no other choice. Frank Thompson was a barber in New York. After his wife became ill, Frank could no longer care for his two children. They arrived at an asylum in Albany, New York, in 1891. Although he could barely read and write, the sorrowful father sent this letter to the superintendent:

> Dear Sir:
>
> as I have not hird from my chldes since they came to you plase I should like to hear from them and how thay like thir home aspecly the boy . . . he will have a hard time of it. I was a shamd to send such dirtty children away bot . . . I could not git them token care of so sente them to you. I hope I may hear from them. I don't now what your rules are inregard to visiting or calling to see children. I should like to call and see them.[4]

Some children and parents did reunite after a time. Sadly, most did not.

## A Prodigy of Crime: Hannah Schoff and the New Century Club of Philadelphia

On a May morning in 1899, Hannah Schoff of Philadelphia opened her newspaper. The headline "A Prodigy of Crime" caught her attention. The story was about a fire set deliberately by an eight-year-old. "I did it to see the fire burn and the engines run," the little girl told the judge.

The seriousness of the crime by one so young had alarmed the court. The judge sentenced the girl to a reformatory. The article explained that the child's parents had died when she was two years old. She had lived in an orphans' home until recently, when the superintendent had placed her as a "helper" in a city boardinghouse. This was the building the child had set aflame.

Schoff had seven children of her own. As a mother, she understood that a child's curiosity often led to mischief, and mischief sometimes led to tragedy. The girl was certainly guilty of starting the fire, but she was not immoral. The punishment the judge had exacted was too harsh. She folded aside her newspaper and decided to tell him so . . . in person.

*Forced labor by adult prisoners is mainly a thing of the past in the United States. Yet just over a century ago, juvenile offenders were used for long hours of manual labor.*

"But what am I to do with her?" the judge responded. "I have no other place to send her, and to tell the truth they do not even want her there, because of the serious nature of the offense!"[5]

Schoff left the court determined to learn about Pennsylvania's laws concerning delinquent children. In the days that followed, she made a surprising discovery. There were no laws. Children were arrested, tried in court, and incarcerated the same as adults. Schoff went to the country prison and found children as young as six locked inside cells. She called them "cages." She visited other county prisons. The situation was much the same. Clearly some of these hundreds of children were rowdies. Others were simply homeless waifs.

Schoff presented her findings to the members of the New Century Club, an organization of women similar to Sorosis. "We know that this is all wrong," she told them, "but how can we make it right?"

The members were wives and mothers. They were not lawyers. They had no experience in public work. "We are not a civic organization. We do not know enough about it to change a thing," they argued.

And yet, just as they could not pass the outstretched hands of the street sweeper without giving a penny, they could not now close their eyes to the injustice of jailing children with adult criminals. That winter, the New Century Club began investigating the justice system. Members visited the Philadelphia Bar Association library and read through volumes of law books. Meanwhile, Hannah discovered that other states, including Illinois, had that very year, 1899, created a children's court. She packed her bags, kissed her children and husband good-bye, and set out to discover for herself what a juvenile justice system was and how it might save Pennsylvania's children.

## The Children's Court: Judge Benjamin Lindsey, Jane Addams, and the Chicago Women's Club

Judge Benjamin Lindsey eyed the trembling boys who stood before him in his Denver courtroom. The charge against them was stealing pigeons from a neighbor's cote. Fifteen years earlier, Ben Lindsey and two of his boyhood friends had also attempted to rob a pigeon roost. Of the three who had plotted the crime, one later died bravely as a soldier and one committed other crimes and went to the penitentiary. As for Ben, he had studied law and become a judge.

The boys standing before him now were guilty as charged, but did that mean they should be sent to a prison with adult robbers, muggers,

*Judge Ben Lindsey earned a reputation as "the kids' judge,"*
*by differentiating between the handling of punishment*
*for children and adults.*

and murderers? Lindsey's own experience told him that a child's sense of right and wrong was not the same as an adult's. He also believed that a troubled home life was the reason many children broke the law.

Judge Lindsey—soon to be called "the kids' judge"—helped to establish a new way of trying to save the children of Colorado: rehabilitation. He focused not on what the juvenile had done but rather on why he or she had done it. He started a process called *probation*. He gave the boys a second chance, but they had to prove themselves by staying out of trouble for a period of months, even years.

In Chicago, Jane Addams was also struggling to make sense of the problem of wayward children. A few years earlier, while traveling in England, she had visited a social settlement called Toynbee Hall. The settlement workers lived in a slum in East London with the purpose of helping their neighbors rise above poverty and distress. When Addams returned to America in 1889, she began a similar settlement on Chicago's West Side. She moved into a home built by a wealthy man, Charles Hull. Shabby wooden tenements and factories surrounded the once-prosperous house. Friends discouraged her from moving into such an unclean, unsafe neighborhood. Addams was determined. She had found her purpose in life. She called her new settlement "Hull House."

The doors to Hull House were always open to her immigrant neighbors, many of whom did not speak English. Soon, they trusted Miss Addams and the other Hull House women with their children. "We were asked to wash newborn babies, to nurse the sick, and to 'mind the children,' " Addams later wrote.[6] She came to understand that a boy who stole coal because his family had none was not a criminal. He was doing the best he could to keep his family from freezing.

"The coal on the wagons, the vegetables displayed in front of the grocery shops, the very wooden blocks in the loosened street paving are a challenge to their powers to help out at home," Addams wrote in *Twenty Years at Hull House*. As for those who stole from department stores or vendors, most were overwhelmed by the grand displays and simply could not help themselves. Many were just looking for playthings. Like Judge

*Jane Addams, shown here with a group of young immigrants, founded Hull House to serve as a community center, meeting place, educational resource, and, above all, a haven for children.*

Lindsey, Addams believed that the court should become a guardian to care for delinquent children and correct their misbehavior.

For the past ten years, the Chicago Women's Club had also been working to improve prison conditions for children and women. These upper- and middle-class women visited police stations and jails. They began a "jail school" for the children. They fought to have female guardians, or matrons, assigned to the cells that held women and children.

Jane Addams and settlement workers of Hull House joined hands with the ladies of the Chicago Women's Club. Together they lobbied, or pressured, Chicago's elected officials to create a children's court. They argued for probation rather than incarceration. As a result of their efforts, Illinois became the first state to pass a juvenile justice law, in 1899.

Inspired by what she had learned on her travels, Hannah Schoff returned to Philadelphia armed with a plan. She hired a lawyer to draft a bill similar to that enacted in Illinois. The women of the New Century Club began lobbying elected officials for changes, just as their sisters in Illinois had done. When the managers of the Eastern House of Refuge in Pennsylvania learned of the proposed reform, they fought against it. If passed, the new law would reduce the number of children in the reformatories. That, in turn, would cut the amount of money the institutions received. The managers feared losing their jobs.

Schoff and the New Century Club defeated the opposition with a blizzard of pamphlets and letters and public speeches. By May 1901, Pennsylvania had its own juvenile justice system.

Not until many years later did Hannah learn the fate of the child who had started the boardinghouse fire. After meeting with Mrs. Schoff, the judge had had a change of heart. He ordered a new trial and placed the girl in another, better "home." She later graduated from normal school and became an assistant school principal.

"And she is what people thought was a Prodigy of Crime," said Hannah Schoff.[7]

I came to what was once a fine, old-fashioned house, but now a dilapidated structure filled with numerous families and termed "not respectable." Through a broken gate and over a short icy path I reached the rear and knocking, was welcomed by Mrs. Blake with a baby in her arms. . . . "Yes, Dick has broke his arm," she answered as she held the door open for me to pass into—what shall we call it?—a bed room, living room, dining room, kitchen,—all in one on the ground floor.

As I first entered, I could not see the boy for the dim light, and crowded room. A huge bed in one corner, boxes, broken chairs, and a miscellaneous collection of things were huddled together; but over by the stove, lying upon a broken lounge, with a chair at the foot to make it long enough, and covered with ragged bedding, was Dick, a boy of fifteen. . . . After a good long visit, I was shown his mother's "conservatory," a few old tomato cans filled with forlorn-looking stalks, yet on some a bit of green, fighting hard against the cold and the darkness from the grimy windows. . . .

As I turned to go, the door was pushed softly open and in came a thin, shivering brown dog. The animal crept up to the lounge and slipped its nose near the boy's face. . . . Leaving the two friends together, I went on to my next calls. . . .

*Mary Baylor, visiting nurse,*
*Washington, D.C. 1906–1907*

## CHAPTER THREE

# ATTACKING THE NEST

M easles, scarlet fever, whooping cough—these were the diseases of childhood. The hot months of summer were particularly dangerous for infants. Each week in cities like Philadelphia, Boston, Baltimore, and Chicago, hundreds of babies died. The editors of the *New York Times* wrote about the crisis in 1876: "There is no more depressing feature about our American cities than the annual slaughter of little children of which they are the scene."[1]

"Annual slaughter" was sensational language—and misleading. The babies had not been murdered. Even so, their deaths were a mystery. At first, public health workers believed the deaths were the result of an inherited disability or physical defect. If not that, then some deadly germ in the air had sickened them. In the 1880s, public health officials began to suspect bacteria was the culprit. This investigation of a dairy farm outside Baltimore, Maryland, provided some clues:

CONFINED IN ONE PLACE were 68 cows. When the stable door was closed there was not enough light to make all of the cows clearly visible. There was no ventilation except that which the stable-owners could not prevent. Vapors and foul odors arose from hot, wet bodies and discharged wastes from the animals. . . . The poor beasts are kept chained up in

*Infant death was rampant in crowded cities, where babies were often left in the care of older siblings while parents worked.*

> such a place for months without fresh air, sunlight or exercise. The
> width of the stalls is barely enough to let the cows lie down. . . .[2]

The milkmaids were no cleaner, the investigators discovered. "If they ever washed their faces and hands it must have been done unintentionally. Filthiness was especially evident by the condition of their hands, which were shaded by layers of manure. . . ."[3]

Samples from uncovered 40-quart (38-liter) milk cans revealed that in 0.06 cubic inch (1 cubic centimeter) of milk were 7,920,00 bacteria. In contrast, samples of milk of the same size taken from cans in another, much cleaner stable revealed 10,000 bacteria.

A process of boiling milk, called *pasteurization,* could kill the harmful bacteria. But the process was new and not widely accepted. City and state inspectors could ensure that dairies were kept cleaner, but inspectors must be paid and many cities did not have the money.

The milk problem did not go away. During the summer of 1902 in New York City alone, an estimated 1,500 babies died each week. A pamphlet published by the Children's Bureau, a government agency, explained why clean dairies and milk inspectors were not enough to stop the sickness. It said:

> IT IS USELESS to send pure milk into a dirty home to be handled by an ignorant, dirty mother or older child. It is necessary to reach the mothers, not only to teach them how to care for their baby's milk, but also to convince them of the necessity of cleanliness.

Public health workers could continue to treat the symptoms of sickness, or they could discover then eliminate the cause of disease. They could continue to "swat the fly." Or they could "attack the nest."

Sara Josephine Baker and Alice Hamilton chose to attack the nest.

# In "Hell's Kitchen":
## Sara Josephine Baker

Sara Josephine Baker and Alice Hamilton were among the very few female physicians in America at the beginning of the twentieth century. Rather than treating patients in an office or hospital, however, they took their knowledge of medicine into tenements, factories, and sweatshops. Dr. Baker was a medical inspector for New York City. Dr. Hamilton was an industrial investigator in Chicago.

The "nest" Dr. Baker entered was a dangerous neighborhood of breweries and factories along the Hudson River known as "Hell's Kitchen." Criminals lurked in the alleys and along the riverfront, giving the neighborhood its nickname. As a medical inspector, Dr. Baker visited tenement families in an effort to stop the spread of disease. She once described her grim work in "Hell's Kitchen" this way: "I climbed stair after stair, knocked on door after door, met drunk after drunk, filthy mother after filthy mother, and dying baby after dying baby."[4]

Dr. Baker discovered that many tenement mothers simply did not know how to care for a baby. They did not understand that cows' milk could spoil in the days it took to transport it from the dairy farms to the city. They did not know that cooking an infant's food could make it safe or that an infant must be fed at regular times. They did not know what Dr. Baker understood—that filthy water, rotting garbage, and animal droppings bred disease.

Superstitions swirled through the tenements. One young Italian mother whose baby suffered from malnutrition tied a string of coral beads around the baby's wrist, believing the bracelet could make him well again. The "black bottle" was another myth believed by some. If a patient was "too slow in dying," the story went, the hospital doctor gave the patient the black bottle to bring on death. Thus, immigrants feared hospitals. A health inspector might discover a sick child "wrapped in bundles" hidden in a closet so that the public health worker would not take a sick child away.[5]

*Living conditions in New York City's Hell's Kitchen were intolerable by today's legal standards, but in the late 1800s there were no building codes.*

*By visiting the families of infants and young children in their home environments, Dr. Josephine Baker established that parental education could save young lives.*

Dr. Baker attacked the nest in a number of ways. If sick people would not—or could not—come to the hospitals, then the health care workers would go to the sick. She began a program of home visits by trained nurses. Among their duties were to dress wounds and to comfort the sick. They also instructed their families to sweep the floors, empty their bedpans properly, and burn their refuse. The pig in the cellar and the chickens cooped under the kitchen sink must be put outside.

Many mothers who worked left their infants in the care of an older child. These young girls were just as ignorant as their mothers in how to care for a baby. And so Dr. Baker began the Little Mothers League. Girls twelve years and older attended demonstrations and learned how to sterilize dishes, how to make a bed, how to properly pin a diaper, and how to feed and bathe an infant. Girls who attended six classes received a silver badge and a certificate that stated they were "volunteer aides of the Department of Health."

Dr. Baker was planning for the future. One day these girls would become mothers themselves. Other cities, following Dr. Baker's example, began their own visiting nurse programs and Little Mothers Leagues. By 1915, almost 50,000 girls in cities across the country had earned their silver badges.

## Typhoid and Flies in Chicago: Alice Hamilton

Disease threatened all people, adults as well as children. Smallpox and typhoid, in particular, spread like wildfire through city slums. Some people blamed the immigrants. They were dirty and lazy, they complained. Dr. Alice Hamilton had a different point of view. Immigrants who had lived in open country spaces in their homelands—in Italy, Greece, Poland—could not easily adapt to life in America's congested cities, where there were no open spaces. Dr. Hamilton explained:

*Dr. Alice Hamilton established the link between filthy surroundings and insect-borne disease as well as the connection between chemical contamination and disease.*

THOSE OF OUR CITY DWELLERS who come from the country, either on this side of the water or the other, find it hard to understand why they should not do the same things in the city that they did on their farms at home. The keeping of goats, chickens and cows in the city seems perfectly natural to them, even if the premises are a bit crowded. A Greek peasant cannot understand why he should not slaughter his sheep in his back yard or even in his basement, nor why he should not toss the manure out of the stable windows into the nearest open space.[6]

Often the source of filth, and therefore disease, was the fault of the landlords. The landlords were often unknown or difficult to track down. Some tenement families wrote letters like those below to the public health officials:

"DEAR SIR—Would like you to call at———, and it is in a very bad order and Mrs. D is living in their five years and was never cleaned." Another letter read: "Water in hall up to knees, 7 and 8 children in two rooms—bad odor from sinks. Housekeeper says she won't let Board of Health in."[7]

Most of these letters were unsigned. If the landlord knew that tenants were complaining, he might throw them out. Within a day another homeless family was sure to take up the space.

On occasion, the public health officials themselves were to blame for the squalid conditions. Poor immigrants were not yet citizens and could not vote. On the other hand, the landlords and factory owners were more prosperous and therefore powerful. A bribe frequently convinced a health inspector to look the other way.

In the summer of 1902, the latest of a series of a typhoid epidemics infected Chicago. That year, however, the death rate had doubled. Dr.

Hamilton noticed a disturbing pattern. A large percentage of the deaths was within the neighborhood surrounding Hull House. The supply of water and milk to these neighborhoods was no different from others. The infection had to come from some other source. Many tenements in this vicinity had backyard privies open to dust and air, to rats and other vermin. These uncovered privies were not only illegal, they proved to be deadly. Dr. Hamilton collected flies from the area of the foul privies. In the laboratory, she discovered a new link in the cause-and-effect chain of disease: fly-borne infection. She wrote up her report:

LESS THAN HALF of the houses had proper equipment and in many there was absolutely no drainage or sewer connection. Open, undrained vaults into which the discharges of typhoid patients had been thrown, were found in close proximity to kitchen windows, offering every opportunity for fly-borne infection. The disease was at its height during the months of flies and sank with the appearance of frost. . . .[8]

Soon after receiving the report, the city of Chicago took action. They sealed the vaults and fined the landlords whose houses did not comply with the law.

## Publicity and Persuasion: Alice Hamilton, Florence Kelley, Albion Bacon

There were other nests in other cities.

Dr. Hamilton's investigations took her inside paint factories where she found lead dust swirling through the air and "smeared" on the sandwiches of the unsuspecting workers, whose hands were covered with the poison. In match factories, workers who inhaled phosphorus developed a disfiguring disease called "fossy jaw." The poison ate through the jawbone. Just as germs made people sick, so too did chemicals poison the body.

Some factory managers dismissed Dr. Hamilton's claims or made light of the chemical contamination. Anyone who didn't like the working conditions, the managers said, could leave. Angry and frustrated, Dr. Hamilton complained to a friend, "You would think I was inquiring about mosquito bites."[9]

Dr. Hamilton submitted her reports to the federal health authorities who had employed her. She wrote about her investigations in newspaper articles and scientific journals. She gave lectures on the subject of workplace poisons. Although women did not have the power of voting, they had two "weapons" in the war against social injustice: publicity and persuasion. Dr. Hamilton knew this well.

Other women, too, were using publicity and persuasion to attack the nest. They wrote letters, circulated petitions, and published newsletters. Often they won their battles. Many times, they did not.

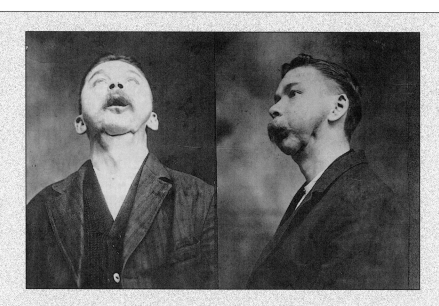

*It took the insistence of Dr. Alice Hamilton for factories to admit the connection between phosphorus (a material used in making matches) and the horribly disfiguring disease called "fossy jaw."*

*Albion Bacon's compassion for those forced to live in slums inspired her to successfully battle for legislation monitoring housing for the poor.*

In Evansville, Indiana, Albion Bacon wrote legislation that required landlords to add windows to their tenement buildings. She was not a lawyer or a physician or a factory inspector. She was simply a mother and a member of a women's club. Evansville was not nearly as large a city as Chicago and yet it, too, had slums. "The conditions made me literally sick," Albion said. "I would lie awake at night and see . . . babies crawling in the filthy yards. I could feel the wind through the cracked walls."[10]

She approached the mayor. "We should have a city ordinance for tenements," she said. The buildings being constructed must allow for light and air so as to prevent the spread of disease. To her surprise, the mayor agreed. He further bewildered her by telling her to write the ordinance herself.

Bacon had never written legislation before. She soon learned how. She wrote not only a city ordinance but also legislation for a state law to address housing for the poor. She traveled to Indianapolis, the state capital, to present her bill. Never before had she been inside the capitol building. Few women had, except as spectators. "I knew it as a seething mass of men. I was badly frightened," she admitted. "I felt so little. The place seemed made for giants."[11]

Albion Bacon was a small woman, no taller than five feet. In her own way, she was herself a giant. For when the tally was taken, her bill on housing for the poor had passed by a single vote.

*Temperance advocate Carry Nation speaks while holding a
Bible and a hatchet, the former serving as her inspiration,
and the latter as a means to destroy bar fixtures and stock.*

## CHAPTER FOUR

# THE WHITE RIBBON WOMEN

Water is much cheaper,
And much more healthy too,
And never makes a man a fool—
Which liquors often do.

Cold water never caused man
In the gutter to be found,
And never, as I know of,
to feel upward for the ground.

*Temperance hymn*

O n the day of her wedding, Carry Moore's husband-to-be was intoxicated with rum. Dr. Charles Gloyd continued drinking in the months following the marriage. Although he did not physically harm his wife, Carry suffered emotionally. The doctor worked less and stayed out more. They had little to eat. "Wrapped in a dingy shawl," her biographer wrote, "she took to flapping around Holden [Missouri], at all hours," looking for the husband too drunk to find his way home.[1] When Mr. Moore learned of his daughter's unhappy situation, he traveled to Holden and convinced Carry to return home with him. Six months later, Dr. Gloyd died from alcoholism.

Carry was now a widow with an infant daughter and no money. David A. Nation was also a widower, almost twenty years older than Carry. She had married Dr. Gloyd for love. Now she needed someone to save her and her daughter from the poorhouse. David needed someone to manage his home. Their wedding was one of convenience. Carry seemed to like most her new husband's name, for upon marriage she became Carry A. Nation. She had always been religious. Now she believed that God had chosen her to "carry a nation" to sobriety.

In the years that followed, Carry A. Nation would become one of the most famous—and most ridiculed—crusaders in the history of the women's temperance movement. So controversial a character was Carry A. Nation that temperance women—also called "white ribboners"—did not accept her as one of their own.

## The Laws of the Country: Clarina Howard Nichols

Women had few legal rights. Once married, her possessions including herself and her future children, became the property of her husband. Her fate was entwined with his deeds. If he were a good and prosperous man, then her life too might be equally good and prosperous. On the other hand, if he were a drunkard, he put the lives of his wife and children at great risk. In most states, there were no laws to protect a woman from a drunkard husband who spent all his money on tankards of ale rather than food for the children or who beat his wife. Even so, women found other ways to save one another.

In Baraboo, Wisconsin, a newspaper reported that "three rum-drinking men abused their wives by beating them, turning them out of doors at dead of night, until their wives thought that death would be preferable to their present life." The women in the community came to the rescue of the suffering wives. They entered several liquor-selling establishments in Baraboo and smashed the liquor bottles and barrels.[2]

The newspapers did not report on what happened a week or a month later when the saloons and drugstores restocked their whiskeys. Perhaps the husbands stopped drinking the ardent spirits—liquor. Most likely, they did not. Alcohol was addictive. Perhaps the beaten wives found courage to leave their husbands. Again, most likely, they did not. Clarina Howard Nichols, a favorite speaker at women's rights meetings, explained why.

THE LAWS OF THIS COUNTRY have bound her hand and foot, and given her up to the protection of her husband. They have committed her soul and body to the protection of the husband, and when he fails from imbecility, misjudgment, misfortune, or intemperance, she suffers. . . . If intemperance did not invade our homes and tear them from over our heads; if it did not take from us our clothing, our bread, the means for our own self development, and for the training of our children in respectability and usefulness; if it did not take our babes from our bosoms, I would not stand here.[3]

## Rum and Ridicule

Temperance societies had begun forming early in the nineteenth century with the specific purpose of limiting the use of alcohol. Most of these societies were religious. Their members prayed, often in front of saloons, for the salvation of the poor sinners inside. Some groups became violent, like the ladies in Baraboo. They entered saloons and smashed the windows and whiskey barrels.

Decades later, following the end of the American Civil War, the liquor industry began to expand rapidly. In part, this was due to the growth of cities. A single city block might have as many as a dozen saloons. By the late 1800s, Americans were spending more for alcoholic beverages than they spent on meat or on public schools.[4]

The growth of the liquor industry and the growing number of educated women who favored women's rights resulted in a new temperance movement. The Women's Christian Temperance Union (WCTU), founded in 1874, was created "by women for women." The old tactics of joint smashing gave way to new strategies. Women learned about constitutional law. They organized marches. They gave public speeches and held rallies. The WCTU opposed the use of alcohol. But the WCTU was about much more than ardent spirits. It became a political platform arguing for women's equality.

To symbolize their mission and their unity, the temperance women wore white ribbons. White held all the prisms of the rainbow, and therefore white represented all women from all walks of life. The "white ribboners" were reformers, not "joint smashers."

At first, as with the women's clubs first organized by Jane Cunningham Croly, many in society did not take the white ribboners seriously. Newspapers, in particular, derided them. They were old maids. They were shrews. In reporting on a temperance parade, editor James Watson Webb of the *New York Courier* focused on the unattractiveness of the women. He wrote:

> ANTIQUATED AND VERY HOMELY FEMALES made themselves ridiculous by parading the streets in company with hen-pecked husbands. . . . Shameless as these females—we suppose they were females—looked, we should really have thought they would have blushed as they walked the streets to hear the half-suppressed laughter of their own sex and the remarks of men and boys.[5]

To be taken seriously, the white ribbon women had to do more than ignore the lewd comments of bystanders and reporters. They formed a committee to explore how to "influence the press." They published pamphlets on how to speak in public and how to organize a meeting. They encouraged members to use "visual" persuasion by creating banners and symbols to decorate a lecture hall during temperance meetings.

By the 1880s, the tone of the press toward the temperance movement had begun to change. Perhaps it was the women themselves who had developed as speakers. Perhaps it was the mood of the times. The temperance movement was growing rapidly. By the end of the century it had become the largest single women's movement in America's history, larger even than Jane Croly's General Federation of Women's Clubs.

*The determination of the Women's Christian Temperance
Union is evinced by these four demonstrators huddled outside
a business that sold liquor in Mount Vernon, Ohio, in 1873.*

*Frances Willard, WCTU president, wears the white ribbon that identifies her as a reformer, not one of the more unruly "joint smashers" of the Carry Nation ilk.*

## The First Saloon: Frances Willard

Frances Willard was a redheaded tomboy who cut her hair short and told everyone to call her Frank. She didn't understand why she and her sister had to stay at home while her brother and father rode off in the wagon to vote. "Shall we ever be anybody, know anything, or go anywhere?" she complained.

As a young woman, Frank eventually left her family's farm along the Rock River in Janesville, Wisconsin, to go to college. She became a successful teacher, and later, the president of Evanston College for Ladies. Many years later, she shocked her friends by leaving her career in education to work for the WCTU. The day Willard made up her mind was the day she entered her first saloon, a place called Sheffner's in Pittsburgh, Pennsylvania. She later described the experience in detail:

I HAD NO MORE IDEA of the inward appearance of a saloon than if there had been no such place on earth. I knew nothing of its high, heavily-corniced bar, its barrels with the ends of all pointed towards the looker-on, each barrel being furnished with a faucet; its shelves glittering with decanters and cut glass, its floors thickly strewn with saw-dust, and here and there a round table with chairs—nor of its abundant fumes, sickening to healthful nostrils. The tall, stately lady who led us, placed her bible on the bar and read a psalm. . . . Then we sang "Rock of Ages" as I thought I had never heard it sung before, with a tender confidence. . . . It was strange, perhaps, but I felt not the least reluctance, and kneeling on that saw-dust floor, with a group of earnest hearts around me, and behind them, filling every corner and extending out into the street, a crowd of unwashed, unkempt, hard-looking drinking men, I was conscious that perhaps never in my life, save beside my sister Mary's dying bed, had I prayed as truly as I did then. . . .

The next day I went on to the West and within a week had been made president of the Chicago W.C.T.U.[6]

Within a short time, the WCTU elected Willard their national president. Under her leadership, the movement developed programs on several aspects of women's rights—kindergartens, prison reform, alcohol education for youth in the schools. Willard's motto was "Do everything." Smashing saloons was *not* what she had in mind.

## Carry's First "Joint": Carry A. Nation

In 1901, David Nation divorced his wife, Carry, who had become something of a fanatic. According to an interview in the Topeka, Kansas, *Journal*, the unhappy husband said "every time a tornado came along she would go into the backyard and pray that it would clean out every saloon in Medicine Lodge."[7]

What the tornadoes did not accomplish, Carry A. Nation did.

In 1880, the state of Kansas had passed a law prohibiting the sale of liquor except for medicinal purposes. That didn't slow the consumption of alcohol. "Daily sufferers" entered drugstores for a dose of whiskey. To accommodate their "patients," some druggists set up planks as makeshift bars. Saloons continued to sell liquor openly and often without consequences.

One Saturday, armed with an umbrella, Nation and another woman marched to Mart Strong's place of business. A crowd followed, expecting trouble or at least some amusement. "Men and women of Medicine Lodge," Nation shouted to the crowd, "this is a joint!"

First, the two women sang a temperance hymn. Then they entered the saloon. Perhaps they wished to continue singing to the men at the bar. Perhaps they meant only to kneel and pray. Given her fiery insults of the past toward anyone she suspecting of drinking, most likely Nation's intentions were to smash Strong's joint to smithereens. Before she got the chance, Strong physically tossed the white-haired woman out the swinging doors and into the street. She got to her feet and charged. Strong "stiff-armed" her in the chest. She fell backward into the street again.

The crowd swelled to many hundred before the marshal finally stopped the brawl. He threatened to take Nation "off the streets."

Now she turned her wrath on him. "You want to take me, a woman whose heart is breaking to see the ruin of these men, the desolate homes and broken laws, and you a constable oath-bound to close this man's unlawful business. Why don't you do your duty?"

The crowd took Carry's side. "Do your duty!" they chanted. Strong hurried inside and barricaded his doors. The men at the bar ran out the back, chased over the fence by irate women who screamed after them, "Drunkard! Drunkard!"[8]

The debacle ended. Soon after, the marshal did his duty and shut down Strong's illegal "joint." Despite her bruises, her victory in Medicine Lodge gave Carry A. Nation confidence that her work was

God's work. She traveled from city to city, smashing joints with bricks and rocks, hammers and axes. She did not escape unharmed from these crusades. The crowds that always formed frequently assaulted her. They threw eggs. They knocked her down and kicked her. Prostitutes, who earned their living inside the saloons, beat her with brooms and horse-whips. Police arrested her on at least thirty occasions. Each time released from jail, she went back to her old ways.

"Oh, I tell you, ladies," she once said, "you never know what joy it gives you to start out to smash a rumshop."[9]

## The Sisters' Next Step

Both Carry A. Nation and Frances Willard worked toward the same goal: the abolition of alcohol. Although their motivations and their methods differed dramatically, both women were in their own way "radicals." Nation was violent to the point of being an embarrassment to the women's temperance movement. Willard challenged those same women by focusing on women's rights, including the right to vote.

Nation's weapon was an ax. She carried miniature axes in her purse to sell as souvenirs. Willard's weapon was the ballot. She had never lost her childhood wish that a woman—any woman—could one day be somebody, know something, and go someplace. Especially the polling place.

Many white ribbon ladies could not support Willard on this critical issue of suffrage. We do not want the ballot in order to be like men, she argued. She urged the women to consider the greater good. Until women had power over the laws that controlled their lives, they were not free and they were not safe. "Sisters," she said, "we have no more need to be afraid of the step ahead of us than of the one we have just taken."[10]

*The separation between colored and white was everywhere, even in publicly funded facilities such as transport and beaches.*

## CHAPTER FIVE

# LIFTING AS WE RISE

It is the women of America—black and white—who are to solve this race problem, and we do not ignore the duty of black women in the matter. They must arouse, educate, and advance themselves. The white woman has a duty in the matter also. She must no longer consent to be passive. We call upon her to take her stand.

*Josephine St. Pierre Ruffin, 1894*

hen Ida. B. Wells was twenty-two years old, a conductor for the Chesapeake and Ohio Railroad forcefully removed her from the ladies' train car. She had refused to sit in the smoker, which was labeled for "colored people." Segregating whites and blacks was a common practice, especially in the southern United States. Local laws that limited the rights of African Americans were called Jim Crow laws. Wells sued the railroad for violating her right for separate but equal transportation. She won her case. A higher court later overturned the ruling.

At the time, Wells was still teaching school in Memphis, Tennessee. She had also begun to write news stories. In one controversial story, she criticized the school board for which she worked. The schools and books for black children, she wrote, were inferior to those the city provided for white children. As a result of that story, she lost her teaching job.

Wells was not afraid of taking risks. She also had come to realize that her value as an individual was not as a teacher but as a journalist. Through her writing, she could expose social injustices. Wells launched her own Memphis newspaper and called it the *Free Speech*.

# The Murder of Thomas Moss:
## Ida B. Wells

The fight began over a game of marbles. According to Ida B. Wells, some white boys and some black boys did not agree on who had won the game. They began fighting. Soon, the boys' fathers—both white and black—entered the fray.

The neighborhood where the fight occurred was a section of Memphis along the streetcar line known as "The Curve." Recently, Thomas Moss and two partners had opened a store there called the People's Grocery Company. Moss's business was competition for another store owned by a white grocer. Rumors circulated that some of the whites were planning revenge on the People's Grocery Company.

That Saturday night, Moss armed several men and posted them in the rear of his store. As Moss was locking up for the night, shots rang out. Moss's men had wounded three men trying to enter the store. What began as an argument among children now exploded into racial hatred. The morning newspaper reported that the wounded men were white officers of the law, shot while doing their duty. The reporter described Moss's store as a place of gambling and other evils. The three wounded men would recover. Still, the sheriff accused Moss and his two partners of sparking a race riot and arrested them. On March 9, 1892, a mob broke into the prison. They abducted the men, took them to a wooded area, and hanged them.

Wells had been out of town when she learned of the Memphis lynchings. She was angry and grief-stricken.. "Everybody in town knew and loved Tommie (Moss)," said Wells. He and his wife were her best friends. "He believed, with me, that we should defend the cause of right and fight wrong wherever we saw it."[1]

Wells returned to Memphis and began her own investigation of the lynchings. Moss and his partners had struggled with their captors, she learned. They had been tortured prior to being hanged. One man's eyes had been gouged out. As for Moss, witnesses claimed he had begged for his life, not for his own sake but for the sake of his children.

*Ida B. Wells-Barnett's lifelong anti-lynching crusade put her life in danger, but her exposés nearly put an end to these brutal killings.*

Wells began to write. Moss and his partners had not been lynched because they had been found guilty of a crime, she reported. They had been murdered because they were successful black businessmen. She quoted Tommie's final words: "Tell my people to go west. There is not justice for them here." In her article Wells also encouraged the colored families to leave Memphis. "We are outnumbered and without arms," she wrote. "There is only one thing left that we can do—leave a town which will neither protect our lives and property, nor give us a fair trial, but takes us out and murders us in cold blood."[2]

For those who stayed in Memphis, she urged them to boycott the services provided by white-owned businesses. Among these service were the streetcars. Wells's words were indeed a powerful weapon. Hundreds of families left Memphis. Many hundreds more stopped riding the streetcars. The owners of the transportation company asked Wells to call off the boycott. She refused. Nor did she quit her investigations.

Now she began digging into the police records on lynching from the past ten years. What she discovered shocked her. White racists claimed that lynching was a justified punishment for black men who assaulted white women. Some assaults had occurred, but Wells revealed that mobs had tortured and lynched men for many "other causes," none of which were serious enough for a death sentence. These included "sheltering a fugitive, disputing a white man's word, dating a white woman, defending themselves against whites, or just acting "troublesome."[3] Not only men but also women and children had died from lynch mob violence.

Wells published her stories in the *Free Speech*, fully expecting some "cowardly retaliation from the lynchers," she said. Again, she was prepared for the consequences. "I felt one had better die fighting against injustice than to die like a dog or rat in a trap."[4]

One night when Wells was again out of town, a mob broke into the office of the *Free Speech*. They had vowed to lynch on Court Square the "black scoundrel" who had written the repulsive stories. Not finding Wells, they instead destroyed the newspaper office.

Wells never returned to Memphis. In Chicago, she continued researching and publishing anti-lynching stories and demanding federal action—an anti-lynching law. Mob violence had destroyed the *Free Speech*. But it could not silence Ida B. Wells.

## For the Benefit of the Race: Josephine St. Pierre Ruffin

Missouri editor James W. Jacks thought Ida. B. Wells was a dangerous woman. To discredit her anti-lynching campaign, he wrote a scathing editorial accusing all black women of immorality: ". . . The women are prostitutes and are natural thieves and liars," he wrote.[5]

Attacks upon the character of the Negro race were not new. His letter had an effect opposite of what he had intended, however, for the times were changing. Like their white sisters, many middle- and upper-class black women had gone to college. They, too, had formed clubs and social settlements, created kindergartens, and built schools. Now, all across America, educated black women rose to make a stand against the slander of their race.

Josephine St. Pierre Ruffin was the president of the Woman's Era Club, a black organization in Boston. In 1895, she called for a national convention of colored women. Just as Jane Cunningham Croly had organized the General Federation of Women's Clubs, now St. Pierre Ruffin helped to form the first-ever national alliance of black women. They called themselves the National Association of Colored Women (NACW). Their goal was to "lift the race" as they themselves had risen.

"Too long have we been silent under unjust and unholy charges," said St. Pierre Ruffin in her opening address. "It is 'most right,' and our boundless duty to stand forth and declare ourselves and principles to teach an ignorant suspicious world that our aims and interests are identical with those of all aspiring women."[6]

A year later, the NACW elected as their president Mary Church Terrell. She was thirty-three years old, and married to the first black judge appointed to a municipal court. Her father was a wealthy, influential man in Memphis, where she had grown up. Tommie Moss had been a childhood friend of hers, as well. His murder deeply shook her faith in her religion and in people. How could good Christians, she asked, allow such terrible injustices as lynching without raising a voice in protest? When called upon to lead the colored women of America, she could not refuse. It was both an honor and an obligation.

Judge Terrell's friends warned him not to allow his wife "to wade too deeply into public affairs." The judge did not listen to his well-meaning friends. He encouraged his wife to accept the invitations she had received to travel around the country and speak about the progress of the race.

Few women traveled alone. As a black in the South, Mary could not travel, dine, or lodge in the same facilities as whites. She faced also the racist attitudes expressed by editor Jacks—black women were not ladies and should not be treated as such. She would be speaking to large crowds of people. Her name would appear in newspapers and pamphlets. She would demonstrate by example that black women were not inferior to white women. Therein lay the danger. Lynch mobs had murdered many hundreds of her people for "acting superior."

Mary's hesitation greatly irritated her husband. "When so few colored women had been fortunate enough to complete a college course," he said, "it was a shame for any of them to refuse to render any service which it was in their power to give."[7]

He was right, of course. "Lifting as we rise" was the foundation on which the NACW had been formed. Despite the dangers, Mary Church Terrell began her lecture tour.

## A Night in Texarkana: Mary Church Terrell

For fifteen years, Terrell traveled and spoke to crowds of men and women. She used the same tools as women before her had used—publicity and persuasion. During one long train journey to Paris, Texas, she believed her worst fears for her safety were about to come true.

The agent who had sold Mary a ticket in Louisiana assured her the train would take her directly to her destination. Once aboard, however, the conductor informed her that she must disembark in Texarkana for the evening and take another train the next morning. Mary was bewildered. Where would she spend the night? Her best hope was to find a boardinghouse for colored people, but Mary did not know anyone in Texarkana.

The conductor ordered a porter to carry her luggage to the hotel across the street. It was a fine hotel, Mary could see, but it was for white people only. Still, she followed the porter into the hotel and asked for a room.

"I had been sitting by an open window in a common coach that hot day passing through Louisiana, while the smoke and dust were covering

*As a graduate of Oberlin College in 1884, Mary Church was among the first black women to complete a college education. When elected the first president of the National Association of Colored Women (NACW), she addressed issues ranging from lynching, Jim Crow, suffrage, and the plight of rural women.*

me with several coats of smudge," she said. Perhaps that is why the conductor had assumed Mary to be a white woman. Perhaps that is why, too, the hotel clerk handed Mary the room key without questioning her color.

She ate a hasty meal, then hurried to her room. Even so, she could not rest. She registered at the hotel under her own name and now realized her mistake. What if someone recognized her name? What if a colored waiter told the management who she was? She remembered then that someone had told her that Texarkana was "the first city in the South in which a colored man had been burned to death."

"I trembled with apprehension and fear," Mary said. No doubt, memories of her friend Tommie Moss rose before her. He, too, had been taken in the night. Negroes had been killed for acting superior. Despite these troubling thoughts, Mary finally fell asleep.

Sometime during the night, a loud noise woke her. She lay still and did not answer. Had they come for her?

The second knock was louder, more insistent than the first. Mary looked about her room for some means of escape. A door led to a small veranda above the street. "I hastily resolved that I would rush to the little balcony and jump. . . . If that did not kill me, I argued, it might stun me enough to prevent me from being so sensitive to pain as I would otherwise be," she said.

Again, the person knocked hard on the door. This time, Mary answered. "What do you want?"

"Lady," came a voice. "Did you ring for a pitcher of water?"

"No, I did not!"

She heard the footsteps outside her door move away. Mary sighed with relief. No one bothered her the rest of the night. [8]

## CHAPTER SIX

# THE AGITATORS

In jail, as one empty hour succeeds another, you realize more keenly the years that women have struggled to be free and the tasks that they have been forced to leave undone for lack of power to do them.

*Katharine Fisher, November 1917*

At the dawn of the twentieth century, women still did not have the right to vote. The suffragist movement was in what some women called "the doldrums." New leaders were needed. Carrie Chapman Catt and Alice Paul stepped forward.

Catt belonged to the National American Women Suffrage Association (NAWSA). Her strategy was to work state by state for the passage of referenda favorable to suffrage. Eventually, she argued, Congress would have no choice but to debate then pass a national amendment to the Constitution granting all women in all states the right to vote.

Alice Paul had a different strategy. Her ideas were bold, controversial, and downright dangerous.

## The Suffragists' Parade of 1913: Rebecca Hourwich Reyher

For months, Alice Paul and fellow suffragist Lucy Burns had been planning a mass demonstration in the nation's capital. With nine bands, more than twenty floats, and five thousand marchers, it would be a suf-

65

fragists' parade unlike any other. Paul intended to wake up America. She scheduled the parade for March 3, one day before the inauguration of Woodrow Wilson, the newly elected president. Wilson and his Republican party had not spoken in favor of women's suffrage. Paul intended to pressure him and his party into doing so.

Thousands of women from across the country traveled to Washington, D.C., for the grand event. On March 3, Woodrow Wilson arrived in Washington by train. Union Station was fairly deserted. Where are all the people? he reportedly asked. His aides told them that they were watching the suffragists' parade.

Leading the parade was a lawyer named Inez Mulholland. She rode a white horse. Her costume included a long, flowing white cape. She wore no hat and her hair hung loose below her shoulders. She looked like a character from ancient Greek mythology. Other characters were also in costume: "Liberty" with a robe of stars and stripes; "Justice," "Charity," "Peace," and "Hope" were represented, also dressed in flowing robes and scarves. As the parade began, the suffragists set free a dove of peace.

The committee had organized marchers into sections. First came women from foreign countries that had recently granted women the right to vote. Next came the "pioneers" from America's western states that had also granted women state suffrage. Then came the women themselves: nurses dressed in uniform, homemakers, farm wives, lawyers, even actresses of the stage and the new motion picture industry. Negro women marched too, but parade organizers insisted that they march in the last section so as not to offend delegates from the southern states. Mary Church Terrell and her followers agreed. Ida B. Wells did not. Years earlier she had fought the railroad against segregation. She would not allow the suffragists to segregate her now. As the parade proceeded from the Capitol Building down Pennsylvania Avenue, Ida stepped from the sidelines and defiantly joined the white women's delegation from Illinois.

*More than half a million people packed Pennsylvania Avenue in Washington, D.C., to witness the Suffragette Parade. Inez Mullholland (inset) in her long white cape and flowing hair looked like a goddess from Greek mythology at the head of the parade.*

The parade route would take the marchers past the White House to the Treasury Building. Trouble began, however, before the marchers had gone many blocks.

A half million people had come to witness the spectacle. Not all were suffrage supporters. Angry spectators chided the men who marched. "Where are your skirts?" they sneered. The crowds surged at the ropes meant to hold them back. The Secretary of War ordered army cavalry into the streets to control the crowd.

From where she stood on her float, dressed as a Southern belle, Rebecca Hourwich Reyher could hear the jeers and shouts of the crowd. Years later, she described the scene:

IT WAS REALLY a riotous, menacing crowd. Men on the street were insulting and obscene, and wanted to do injury to the women who were parading on foot. Other men, in some way, wanted to provoke what is today called an "incident." We were wearing wide [hoop] skirts, and before I realized it, as we passed by, men were trying to lift those skirts. . . . One man broke through the barriers and tried to lift one of the girl's skirts and pull her off the float. At that point a man with a walking stick, a fine stereotype of a gentleman, rushed up indignantly, and waving his stick, threatened if the hoodlum didn't move on immediately, he would break his back. The disturber slunk away.[1]

The angry spectators attacked many of the marchers. Ambulances tried to navigate through the crowds. More than three hundred people were injured. Even after the parade ended, Rebecca was not safe.

I DON'T REMEMBER which way I went, but I remember that we were warned by the police as we headed for home in our costumes to get home as fast as we could because the streets were not safe for women who were wearing the signia of the parade. . . . I had never before, or after, seen any kind of roughhouse on Washington streets. The parade inspired it, no question about. . . .

It was the only time I have ever been terrified on the streets of Washington, or anywhere.[2]

A few days later, the United States Senate held an investigation into the "mistreatment of the marchers." According to Senate records, one witness complained, "There would be nothing like this happen if you would stay at home."

## Picketing the President: Ernestine Hara Kettler

Alice Paul believed that agitating for equal rights was an effective strategy for increasing awareness of the suffragist cause. Carrie Chapman Catt did not agree. Women ran the risk of alienating supporters if they demonstrated too wildly, she argued.

Alice Paul, Lucy Burns, and other "militant" suffragists broke away from the mainstream and formed their own organization, the National Women's Party (NWP). They held street corner meetings. They stood on the seats of an automobile and shouted through a bullhorn to the crowd. Write to your congressmen and senators, they bellowed. Demand that women get the vote! High school teacher and suffragist Mabel Vernon once heckled President Wilson when he spoke in public. "What are you going to do about women's rights?" she shouted. When the president ignored her, she shouted again, "Answer, Mr. President." Officers of the secret service escorted her away.[3]

When war began in Europe in 1915, President Wilson declared to the world that the United States was neutral and would not enter the fighting. The president took no side on the issue of women's suffrage, either.

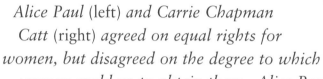

*Alice Paul* (left) *and Carrie Chapman Catt* (right) *agreed on equal rights for women, but disagreed on the degree to which women could go to obtain them. Alice Paul picketed the White House and spent time in jail, while Carrie Chapman Catt took what Ms. Paul might term a more passive "ladylike" approach.*

A few years later, when the president still had not given his support to suffrage, Paul realized that she and the NWP had to increase pressure on the him. And she knew just how to do it.

No one had ever picketed the White House for a political cause. The decision to do so was both serious and difficult. The leaders of the NWP debated it for weeks before finally deciding. "When you start, you have to be prepared to come through for a long time or it is ineffective," Paul explained. She also warned her followers that they must be prepared to go to jail. They were.

The picketing began in January. Four women at a time stood outside the White House gates. They carried placards. One read: "Mr. President, how long must women wait for liberty?"

*Like their sisters before them who stood vigil in the cold outside of saloons, these women braved the elements to picket a much more politically significant venue, the White House.*

When President Wilson traveled from the White House in his car, he often acknowledged the suffragists with a nod or a tip of his hat. The pickets continued for twenty-four hours a day, always in groups of four women.

The arrests began in June. Ernestine Hara Kettler had traveled all the way from Los Angeles to participate in the White House picketing. She was twenty-one years old, unmarried, and idealistic. She knew the risks. Each woman had strict instructions, she said, to ignore the bystanders who would gather at the gates to heckle them.

"There were always men and women standing out there harassing," she said. "The police left us alone, but when the crowd got too noisy and the police couldn't get rid of them, then they hauled us in for obstructing traffic. . . ."

In court, the women argued in their own defense. "We were very bold," Ernestine said. "We told them we couldn't possibly obstruct traffic. There was only one row of us, only four of us. There was plenty of room."

The judge sentenced the women to three days in jail. But already, another group of four women were picketing the White House gates.

"That's what drove the policemen crazy," said Ernestine; "they saw no end to the number of women who were picketing."[4]

Week after week, month after month, the picketing continued. President Wilson wrote to his daughter in June that the suffragists seemed unwilling to give up. He was right.

## Protest at the Occoquan Workhouse: Alice Paul

Alice Paul took the same risks as her demonstrators. On October 20, 1917, she was among the four women arrested for obstructing traffic at the White House gates. The court sentenced her to seven months in prison, an unusually harsh sentence. They placed her with other militant suffragists in the Occoquan Workhouse, across the Potomac River in Virginia.

One of the agitators, Dorothy Day, wrote this about the prison and the treatment of the women taken there:

IT WAS PITCH DARK when we reached the workhouse and were forced by the guards to the superintendent's receiving office. They went out of their way to be rough, pulling us by our arms over the country road

*Alice Paul's arrest by the Washington police does not appear
to be violent in any way, but the prison to which she would
be taken was another story.*

through the dark, and practically throwing us into the room. . . . There was only a single bunk in each cell, but there were so many of us that they put two in each one. . . .

When Lucy Burns was flung into the cell with me she stood by the barred door and began calling to some of the other women to see if they had been injured. She refused to heed the order of the superintendent to "shut up" and he came to the cell, his face livid with rage, and ordered the guards to handcuff her to the bars. She was forced to stand there for several hours with her arms up above her head.[5]

The superintendent put the ringleader Paul in solitary confinement. He would not permit friends or even an attorney to meet with her. Occoquan was a workhouse prison, and the superintendent expected the militant suffragists to do their share of the work. They refused. They sat at the table with their hands folded. They protested in still another way. They refused to eat.

Prison authorities ordered Paul to a psychopathic ward and threatened to place her permanently in an insane asylum if she didn't eat. When threats didn't work, the officials began force feedings. The "operation," as the women suffragists called the force-feeding session, was terrifying. Alice Paul described the ordeal:

WHEN THE FORCE FEEDING was ordered I was taken from my bed, carried to another room and forced into a chair, bound with sheets. . . . Then the prison doctor, assisted by two women attendants, placed a rubber tube up my nostrils and pumped liquid through it into the stomach. Twice a day for a month, from November 1 to December 1, this was done.[6]

Slowly, those on the outside began to learn the truth about what was happening at Occoquan. Carrie Chapman Catt had long believed that

Paul's tactics were not only foolish but harmful to the movement. She did nothing to help her or the other militants imprisoned at Occoquan.

On November 10, thirty-three women picketed the White House to protest the imprisonment of the suffragists. They, too, soon found themselves in the workhouse prison. What happened next became known as a "night of terror." Prison guards beat the women, clubbing one into her cell, chaining another by her wrists to bars over her head and leaving her there through the night. Those beaten required medical care, but received none. The superintendent of Occoquan apparently knew of the violence and did nothing to stop it.

Eventually, through the work of lawyers and perhaps because of the growing negative publicity in the press, the women were released. In January, a district court overturned their sentences. Soon after, President Wilson declared his support for women's suffrage, though it would take another two years for women to win the vote.

Perhaps Paul's militant tactics had worked. Or perhaps, as Catt believed, the time had come when America finally realized that giving women the vote was not a matter of "spheres." It was a matter of social justice.

## CHAPTER SEVEN

# THE PACIFISTS

*In the history of one nation after another, it was the mothers who first
protested that their children should be no longer slain as living sacrifices
upon the altars of the tribal gods. . . . They rebelled against the
destruction of their own children, the waste of the life they had nurtured.*

*Jane Addams, 1931*

The Great War in Europe began with a single assassin's bullet.
The murderer had taken the life of the archduke, heir to the
Austrian-Hungarian empire. By August 1914, Germany was
at war with France and Russia, and Great Britain, in turn,
had declared war on Germany.

Thousands of miles away across the Atlantic Ocean, Jane Addams
was vacationing on the coast of Maine. On an August morning, she saw
a German steamship in Frenchman's Bay. The captain was fearful of cap-
ture and so had sought refuge near land. The huge boat, Addams said,
was alarming to see so close to shore in Maine's peaceful waters.

In adopting a position of neutrality, President Wilson assured the
nation that war in Europe would not reach America's shores. But Jane
Addams remembered the German ship in Frenchman's Bay. This was a
world war and the world's women, she reasoned, might be able to do
something to end the fighting.

For more than sixty years, women had fought for social justice. They
had moved out of the home sphere and into their communities, lobbying
for laws to protect children, the poor, the sick. They had extended their
crusade to the nation in a fight against lynching and Jim Crow laws and
for the rights of women to be free from abusive husbands. Now they
were about to fight for social justice on a grander scale: world peace.

*Women, Jane Addams among them, hold up the banner of the
Women's Peace Movement at a 1914 parade in New York City.*

In January 1915, Jane Addams and Alice Hamilton were among the
3,000 women who met in the Willard Hotel in Washington, D.C., to create the Women's Peace Party. Once again, women were demanding a
voice in the decisions that affected their lives. Those decisions now
included making war.

Women pacifists in Europe invited the Americans to send a delegation
to an International Congress of Women that would be held that summer
in the Netherlands, also a neutral country. The sole purpose of the con-

gress was to discuss how women might negotiate peace among the leaders of the warring nations.

Theodore Roosevelt was no longer the president of the United States, but he was still a respected leader. Although Roosevelt supported women's suffrage, he thought the decision of the Women's Peace Party to go to Europe was silly. The women did not understand the difference between righteousness and wickedness. Men did not fight wars because they thirsted for blood, he argued. They fought because they were taking a stand against evil. Not only would the women fail in their mission, he predicted, but their behavior in meddling in what they simply did not understand was repulsive.

Despite years of women proving themselves as leaders in their community and in the professions, despite reforms they had helped to bring about in health and sanitation and child care, the old argument held sway. Politics and war were men's sphere. Women belonged at home. The women didn't listen. Alice Hamilton wrote to her sister on April 5, 1915:

Dear Agnes,

Will you think me utterly mad when I tell you that I am going over to the Netherlands with Miss Addams and the rest of the Peace delegation. I made up my mind quite suddenly . . . of course, I could not decide really till I knew just how mother would take it . . . But she seems not to worry about it at all. . . .

Yours ever—Alice [1]

A few days later, Dr. Hamilton joined the American delegation. The women posed for a photograph, then boarded a Dutch ship called the *Noordam*. As the ship departed New York harbor, a flag flew from one of the masts. It read simply: "PEACE."

*Jane Addams once again holds a Peace banner, this one destined to fly from the mast of the Dutch ship* Noordam.

# The "Mothers of Men": Mrs. William Lowell Putnam, Alice Hamilton

As the women sailed for Europe, mockery of them began sweeping the newspapers at home. A particularly bitter attack came from Mrs. William Lowell Putnam and appeared in the *Boston Herald*. The Woman's Peace Party, she wrote,

> IS ONE OF THE MOST DANGEROUS movements which has threatened our emotional people for some time. . . . These good women, of whom the most prominent are childless, and many of whom are spinsters against whom no breath of scandal has ever been raised, were lined up together and photographed as "mothers of men" and no one of them saw the absurdity of it all.[2]

Jane Addams was indeed a single woman. She had never married and had no children. Even so, those who respected her for her work often called her "mother." So great was her reputation that the International Congress of Women had elected her to be their president and preside over the meeting in the Netherlands. Mrs. Putnam's remarks were mean-spirited, but so too was the reaction of the British. Once the delegation arrived, they discovered that the British press sarcastically referred to them as "Peacettes."

In all 1,100 women attended the congress. Many came from "belligerent" countries at war, including Germany. Canada, Hungary, Great Britain, Austria, France, Norway, Poland, Belgium, and Sweden all sent delegates. Many women had difficulty securing passports and traveling across the borders of warring countries. Once assembled, they adopted a platform that opposed war and protested the violation of women who were the victims of war. They proposed education of the world's children as a way to prevent future wars. A final task was to appoint two teams of delegates, women who would visit the heads of state of each warring country and personally present their proposals for peace.

The congress had ended, but the women's peace efforts had just begun.

They are attempting the impossible, the American press wrote. Even Dr. Hamilton was dismayed at the task before them. She wrote home on May 5:

J.A. [JANE ADDAMS] IS ONE of the delegates to visit all the countries except Russia and Scandinavia. She wants me to go with her and of course I will. To me it seems a singularly fool performance, but I realize that the world is not all Anglo-Saxon and that other people feel very differently.[3]

On May 7, a German torpedo sank a British ocean liner named the *Lusitania*. Among the 1,200 dead were 128 Americans. The *Lusitania* was not a warship. The Germans had attacked a civilian vessel. The people of Great Britain and America were outraged. Many Americans urged the president to enter the war. Peace seemed further away than ever.

Still, Addams and Hamilton packed their bags and prepared to visit the political leaders of Germany in that country's capital, Berlin. They had come too far to turn back now.

## Peace and Propaganda: Jane Addams, Alice Hamilton

The delegates returned to America on July 5, 1915. They had failed to negotiate peace, but they had succeeded in making their opposition heard. A few days later, Jane Addams addressed a standing-room-only crowd of 3,000 in New York City's Carnegie Hall. She walked on stage to cheers. She told them what she had seen in Europe. She spoke of the battlefields and the soldiers and their families. We had been told that no one in Germany wanted peace, she said, but they had spoken with German men and women who longed for a peaceful solution to the crisis.

Toward the end of her speech, she shared this disturbing information:

> WE WERE TOLD by young men everywhere who had been to the front, that men had literally to be stimulated to a willingness to perform the bloody work of bayonet charges. The English are in such cases given rum; the French, it is said, absinthe; the Germans, more scientifically perhaps, inhalations of ether.

The soldiers required these spirits, she explained, in order to do " the brutal work of the bayonet, such as disemboweling."[4]

America had changed since the war clouds darkened the skies. After the sinking of the *Lusitania*, many viewed the actions of the Women's Peace Party as unpatriotic. Addams's comments at Carnegie Hall seemed equally traitorous. The incident became known as "the bayonet story." It was, Addams admitted, her "undoing." The press turned against her.

"Being a woman," wrote a reporter for the *Phildelphia Inquirer*, "[Addams] can't understand how men can possess sufficient physical courage to charge into a cloud of shot and shell unless 'soused to the gills.' "[5] The *New York City Town Topics* attacked Addams personally, calling her "a silly, vain, impertinent old maid, who may have done good charity work at Hull House, but is now meddling with matters far beyond her capacity."[6]

In April 1917, the United States Congress voted to enter the war. Only one woman served in Congress during that session. Jeannette Rankin was a representative from Montana, the first woman elected to Congress. She cast her vote against war. "The first time a woman had a chance to say no against war she should say it," she later explained. Hers was not the only vote against war but she was greatly outnumbered. The Great War in Europe had enlisted America at last.

*When Jeannette Rankin voted against war with Germany in 1917, she was only one of 56 who opposed U.S. entry into the war.*

The declaration of war by the United States silenced many pacifists. Jane Addams, however, continued to speak. One evening at a meeting in Evansville, Illinois, she addressed a sullen, uneasy audience. She began:

> I AM PRESIDENT of the Woman's Peace Party of America. We believe that the present international situation will have to find some international solution; that one alliance fighting another alliance will never settle it.

Pacifists were not cowards, she said. Instead, they see the need for an international organization where nations both great and small could debate and solve their differences. She was asking her audience to put patriotism aside and think instead of a league of nations and international rights for all.

No one cheered. No one applauded. At last, a gentleman stood up. She recognized him as a old acquaintance, Judge Carter.

"I have been a life-long friend of Miss Addams," he said. "I have agreed with her on most questions in the past—

She interrupted him, smiling. "That sounds as if you are going to break with me, Judge."

"I am going to break," he said.[7]

## The Swamp: Alice Hamilton

Attacks by the media eventually wore Jane Addams down. She experienced "weeks of feverish discomfort." The power and propaganda of the press were at times so overwhelming that Addams felt it "impossible to hold one's own against it."

Alice Hamilton encouraged her. "I want you to keep on saying things even more positively, no matter what you are called, for in the end it will count."

Although she spoke confidently to Addams, Dr. Hamilton was herself distressed at the way people had so misunderstood their intentions. She wrote to her sister:

> IT IS AS IF we had stood at the edge of an awful swamp and seen our friends struggling in it, and the militarists said we must jump in and help them out, and the pacifists said we must try to build a bridge over, though no bridge had ever been built before. . . . The swamp is deeper and more deadly than we knew.[8]

The war ended on November 11, 1918. President Wilson revealed a detailed plan to prevent future world wars. Influenced, in part, by the ideas of Jane Addams and the Women's Peace Party, he hoped to create an international league of nations. The League of Nations was a new world order, an international organization to ensure the rights of all citizens in the world, not just Americans, or Germans, or Belgians. The proposal met with resistance. It was, however, a new and hopeful beginning.

Many years later, in 1931, after the war propaganda had ended, the world recognized Jane Addams's contributions as a social reformer and a pacifist. She received the greatest honor any individual who works for social justice can—the Nobel Peace Prize.

# WINTER WHEAT

This is winter wheat we're sowing,
and other hands will harvest.

*Elizabeth Cady Stanton*

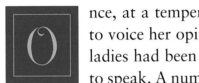nce, at a temperance meeting, Susan B. Anthony attempted to voice her opinion. A gentleman told her to sit down. The ladies had been invited to the meeting to listen, he said, not to speak. A number of years later, during the winter of 1869, Anthony attended a meeting of Jane Cunningham Croly's Sorosis club. The topic of discussion turned to marriage. A lady asked, "Why can't a woman propose marriage? Why must the decision be left to the man?"

This time, Susan B. Anthony could speak freely:

UNDER PRESENT CONDITIONS, it would require a good deal of assurance for a woman to say to a man, "Please, sir will you support me for the rest of my life?" When all avocations are open to woman and she has an opportunity to acquire a competence, she will then be in a position where it will not be humiliating for her to ask the man she loves to share her prosperity. Instead of requesting him to provide food, clothing and shelter for her, she can invite him into her home, contribute her share to the partnership and not be an utter dependent.[1]

Anthony was a much-respected woman. Even so, her response startled the others, for she was suggesting a momentous change in women's role in society.

Anthony's good friend was Elizabeth Cady Stanton. Stanton had grown up with the sad awareness that her father loved her brother more than her. She learned Greek as a child. She studied law in her father's offices. And still he said to her, "If only you were a boy."

In 1892, Stanton addressed Congress in support of an amendment to the Constitution granting women suffrage. "No matter how much women prefer to lean, to be protected and supported," she said, "nor how much men prefer to have them do so, women must make the voyage of life alone, and for safety in an emergency, they must know something of the laws of navigation."[2]

Both Susan B. Anthony and Elizabeth Cady Stanton had worked tirelessly throughout their lives for women's rights, including the right to vote. Neither, however, lived to see the Nineteenth Amendment to the United States Constitution, which guaranteed this right, become law.

In autumn, the farmer plants a crop of wheat that can endure the cold of winter. Come spring, the farmer harvests the crop. Winter wheat nourishes the family until summer's crops ripen. Society's sisters of the nineteenth and early twentieth century were like the farmer. They, too, were sowing winter wheat. Although they did not agree on issues of child care, temperance, or suffrage, although they were not always successful in their reforms, they still believed they could make the world a better place.

Society is made up of people, and people are not constant. Their needs and desires, fears and failures change with time. New problems arise. Old problems persist. What doesn't change is society's need for people to care for one another.

## Crystal Eastman

Crystal Eastman was an infant in 1892, the year Elizabeth Cady Stanton addressed Congress. A generation of women before her had gone to college. They had opened the doors to education for her. Eastman studied law. Like Florence Kelley and Alice Hamilton, she worked for a time in a social settlement. She marched in suffragist parades and picketed the White House with Alice Paul and Lucy Burns. Like Jane Addams, she became a pacifist. She was among the 3,000 women who gathered in the Willard Hotel in 1915 to form the Women's Peace Party. And on November 20, 1920, she was among the 8 million American women who voted for the first time in a national election.

Crystal Eastman had harvested the hard work of women like Susan B. Anthony and Elizabeth Cady Stanton, Sara Josephine Baker and Alice Hamilton, Frances Willard and Ida B. Wells.

But seasons, like society, change. Once more it was autumn. Now it was Eastman's turn to sow the winter wheat for the next generation. She planted the seeds of social justice that created the American Civil Liberties Union, an organization that continues today to fight for the rights of all Americans as stated in the Constitution.

"Women face the future with immense power in their hands," Eastman said soon after Congress passed into law the Nineteenth Amendment. "How will they use it? *The Suffragist* has asked women in various fields of activity to answer the question, What shall women do next? What is Your Answer?"[3]

BOOKS AND ARTICLES

Addams, Jane. *Peace and Bread in Time of War*. New York: Macmillan, 1922.
_____. *Twenty Years at Hull House*. New York: Macmillan, 1912.
_____. "Why Women Should Vote," Frances M. Borkman and Annie G. Poritt, eds. *Woman Suffrage: History, Arguments, and Results*. New York: National Woman Suffrage Publishing, 1915, pp. 131–150.
"Alice Paul Talks: Hunger Striker Describes Forcible Feeding," *Votes for Women, 1848-1921*. Washington, DC: Rare Book and Special Collections Division, Library of Congress.
Baker, Paula. "The Domestication of Politics: Women and American Political Society, 1780–1920." *Unequal Sisters*. New York: Routledge, 1990.
Baylor, Margaret. "The Washington of a Mission Visitor," *Charities and the Commons* XVII, April 1906-October 1906. New York: The Charity Organization Society, pp. 559-562.
Bennett, Helen Christine. *Votes for Women: Selections from the National American Woman Suffrage Association Collection, 1848-1921*. New York: Dodd, Mead, 1915.
Blair, Karen. *The Clubwoman as Feminist: True Womanhood Redefined, 1868-1914*. New York: Holmes and Meier, 1980.
Croly, Jane Cunningham, "Women's Clubs and Their Uses," *The Galaxy* 7:6, June 1869.
Decosta-Willis, Miriam, ed. *The Memphis Diary of Ida B. Wells: An Intimate Portrait of the Activist as a Young Woman*. Boston: Beacon Press, 1995.
Degen, Marie Louise. *The History of the Woman's Peace Party*. New York: Garland, 1972.
Dulberger, Judith A. *"Mother Donit fore the Best: Correspondence of a Nineteenth-Century Orphan Asylum."* Syracuse, NY: Syracuse University Press, 1996.

Foster, Catherine. *Women for All Seasons: The Story of the Women's International League for Peace and Freedom.* Athens, GA: University of Georgia Press, 1989.

Fuller, Margaret. *Women in the 19th Century and Kindred Papers.* Cleveland: John Jewett, 1855.

Grant, Robert. "The Art of Living: The Case of Woman," *Scribner's Magazine* 18:4 (October 1895) pp. 465.

Hamilton, Alice. "The Social Settlement and Public Health" *Charities and the Commons* XVII, April 1906-October 1906. New York: The Charity Organization Society, p. 1037.

Harvey, Sheridan. "Marching for the Vote: Remembering the Woman Suffrage Parade of 1913," *Library of Congress Information Bulletin*, March 1998.

Jones, Beverly Washington. *Quest for Equality: The Life and Writings of Mary Eliza Church Terrell, 1863–1954.* Brooklyn: Carlson, 1990.

Jones, C. Hampson. "The Present Needs of the Milk Supply of Baltimore," *Charities and the Commons* XVI, April, 1906-October 1906, New York: The Charity Organization Society, pp. 499–502.

"Hull House Maps and Papers." *Atlantic Monthly* 77:459 (January 1896), 119–124.

Kelley, Florence, "Persuasion or Responsibility?" *Votes for Women, 1848-1921,* Washington, DC: Rare Book and Special Collections Division, Library of Congress.

Lerner, Gerda, ed. *Black Women in White America.* New York: Vintage Books, 1972.

"Maternity Protection," *Bulletin* (Women's City Club of New York) November 1917, p. 2.

Mattingly, Carol. *Well-Tempered Women: Nineteenth Century Temperance Rhetoric.* Carbondale: Southern Illinois University Press, 1998.

Meckel, Richard A. *Save the Babies: American Public Health Reform and the Prevention of Infant Mortality, 1850-1929.* Baltimore: The Johns Hopkins University Press, 1990.

Millstein, Beth, and Jeanne Bodin. *We, the American Women: A Documentary History.* Englewood, NJ: Jerome S. Ozer, 1977.

"Orders Bowery to Be Cleaned," *Charities and the Commons* XVII, April 1906–October 1906, New York: The Charity Organization Society, p. 1117.

Plante, Ellen M. *Women at Home in Victorian America: A Social History.* New York: Facts on File, 1997.

Scott, Anne Firor. *Natural Allies: Women's Associations in American History.* Chicago: University of Illinois Press, 1991.

Sicherman, Barbara. *Alice Hamilton: A Life in Letters.* Cambridge, MA: Harvard University Press, 1984.

Sklar, Kathryn Kish. *Florence Kelley and the Nation's Work: The Rise of Women's Political Culture, 1830–1900.* New Haven: Yale University Press, 1995.

Taylor, Robert Lewis. *Vessel of Wrath: The Life and Times of Carry Nation.* New York: New American Library, 1966.

Terrell, Mary Church. *A Colored Woman in a White World*. Washington, DC: Ransdell, 1940.

Wells-Barnett, Ida. *Crusade for Justice: The Autobiography of Ida B. Wells*. Chicago: University of Chicago Press, 1970.

Willard, Frances. *Glimpses of Fifty Years: The Autobiography of an American Woman*. Philadelphia: H.J. Smith & Co., 1889.

Williams, Fannie Barrier. "The Club Movement Among Colored Women of America," J.E. MacBready, ed. *A New Negro for a New Century*. Chicago: American Publishing House, 1900, pp. 379–405.

Zangrando, Robert L. *The NAACP Crusade Against Lynching, 1909–1950*. Philadelphia: Temple University Press, 1980.

SELECTED WEB SITES AND
PRIMARY SOURCES ONLINE

American Memory, Library of Congress, http://memory.loc.gov/ammem/amhome.html

Ford, Linda. "Alice Paul and the Triumph of Militancy," home.sprynet.com. Originally appeared in Marjorie Spruill Wheeler, ed. *One Woman, One Vote: Rediscovering the Woman's Suffrage Movement*, 1995.

Matya, Marsha Lakes. "Sara Josephine Baker, Physician and Public Health Worker, 1873–1945," The American Physiological Society, www.the-aps.org

The Suffragists Oral History Project Collection. University of California at Berkeley Library, www.sunsite.berkeley.edu

Women and Social Movements in the United States,.State University of New York at Binghamton. www.womhist.binghamton.edu

# SOURCE NOTES

*Introduction*
1. Sklar, *Florence Kelley and the Nation's Work*, pp. 29–30.
2. Ibid., p. 45
3. Willard, "Address to the National Women's Council," February 1891, "Votes for Women 1848–1921," American Memory, Library of Congress, memory.loc.gov
4. Blair, *The Clubwoman as Feminist*, p. 99.

*Chapter One*
1. John Cunningham, "Memories of Jennie June Croly," American Memory, Library of Congress, memory.loc.gov
2. Harris, "The Complete Education of Females," *New Englander and Yale Review* 11:42 (May 1853), pp. 296–297.
3. Fuller, *Women in the 19th Century and Kindred Papers*, p. 120.
4. Addams, *Twenty Years at Hull House*, p. 64 & p. 78.
5. Decosta-Williams, *The Memphis Diary of Ida B. Wells*, p. x.
6. "I Want," *Scribner's Monthly Magazine*, 21:5 (March 1881), p. 967.
7. Grant, "The Art of Living," *Scribner's Monthly Magazine* 18:4 (October 1895), p. 469.
8. Croly, "Women's Clubs and Their Uses," *The Galaxy* 7:6 (June 1869), p. 901.
9. Blair, p. 99.
10. Croly, p. 901.
11. Croly, p. 903.
12. Blair, p. 115, quoting the *Chicago Record-Herald*, June 7, 1914.

*Chapter Two*
1. Plante, *Women at Home in Victorian America*, p. 107, quoting John H. Young, *Our Deportment*, 1882.

2. From Almshouse to Asylum: Orphans in Allegheny Country," www.clpgh.org

3. "The Making of Thieves in New York," *The Century 1894,* pp. 109–116.

4. Dulberger, '*Mother donit fore the Best,*' p. 30.

5. Bennett, *Votes for Women, 1848-1921,* p. 144.

6. Addams, *Twenty Years at Hull House,* p. 109.

7. Bennett, p. 160.

*Chapter Three*

1. Meckel, *Save the Babies,* p. 11.

2. Jones, C. Hampson, M.D. "The Present Needs of the Milk Supply of Baltimore," *Charities and the Commons* XVI:18 (August 4, 1906), p. 499.

3. Ibid., p. 500.

4. "Sara Josephine Baker, Physician and Public Health Worker 1873–1945," teaching unit developed by The American Physiological Society, www.the-aps.org

5. Sklar, p. 266.

6. "The Social Settlement and Public Health," *Charities and the Commons* XVII (October  1906–April 1907), p. 1037.

7. Dinwiddie, "The Work of New York's Tenement House Department," *Charties and the Commons* XVII (October 1906–April 1907), p. 12.

8. Dinwiddie, p. 1039.

9. Sicherman, *Alice Hamilton: A Life in Letters,* p. 181.

10. Bennett, *Votes for Women, 1848–1921,* pp. 124–125.

11. Bennett, p. 128.

*Chapter Four*

1. Taylor, *Vessel of Wrath,* p. 53.

2. Mattingley, *Well-Tempered Women,* pp. 98–99.

3. Mattingley, p. 35.

4. Women's Christian Temperance Union, www.wctu.org

5. Mattingly, pp. 100–101.

6. Willard, *Glimpses of Fifty Years,* pp. 340–341.

7. As quoted in Taylor, p. 79.

8. Taylor, pp. 82–85.

9. Kansas Historical Society, hs4.kshs.org

10. Merrick, *Old Times in Dixie Land: A Southern Matron's Memories,* p. 145.

*Chapter Five*

1. The account of Thomas Moss's murder as well as Ida's comments on his friendship comes from Wells-Barnett, *Crusade for Justice,* pp. 47–51.

2. Sterling, *Black Foremothers: Three Lives,* p. 791.

3. Zangrando, *The NAACP Crusade Against Lynching,* p. 4.

4. Newkirk, "Ida B. Wells-Barnett: Journalism as a Weapon Against Racial Bigotry" as reprinted online at www.hartford-hwp.com

5. Williams, Lillian Serece, "Records of the National Association of Colored Women's Clubs, 1895–1992," University Publications of America, www.lexis-nexis.com/academic

6. "Address of Josephine St. P. Ruffin," *Woman's Era*, pp. 13-15, as reprinted online at womhist.binghampton.edu.

7. Terrell, *A Colored Woman in a White World*, p. 50

8. Terrell, pp. 299–302.

*Chapter Six*

1. Reyher's account comes from Suffragists Oral History Project Collection at the University of California, Berkeley; www.sunsite.berkeley.edu

2. Ibid.

3. Vernon's account from Suffragists Oral History Project Collection, www.sunsite.berkeley.edu

4. Kettler's account comes from Suffragists Oral History Project Collection, ibid.

5. Day, Chapter Seven, *From Union Square to Rome*, as posted on www.catholic-worker.org

6. "Alice Paul Talks," *Votes for Women, 1848–1921*.

*Chapter Seven*

1. Hamilton, *A Life in Letters*, p. 184.

2. Degen, The History of the Woman's Peace Party, p. 73.

3. Hamilton, p. 190.

4. Degen, p. 111

5. Degen, p. 113

6. Hamilton, p. 194.

7. Degen, p. 200.

8. Hamilton, p. 206.

*Epilogue*

1. Ida Husted Harper, *Life and Work of Susan B. Anthony*, Chapter XIX, Collection published, 1898–1908.

2. Stanton, "Solitude of Self," speech delivered to Congress, January 18, 1892.

3. Eastman, "What's Next?" *The Suffragist* VII (November 1920), pp. 278–279.

Page numbers in *italics* refer to illustrations.